Thoughts of Mine Becoming Thoughts of Yours

Jessica Stewart

BookLeaf Publishing

Presentation by *BookLeaf Publishing*

Web: www.bookleafpub.com

E-mail: info@bookleafpub.com

ISBN: 9789357210850

First edition 2022

DEDICATION

This book is dedicated to anyone who has made me think, brought enough emotions to feel, and to the ones who are brave enough to live your truth!

The Empath Bleeds

Give, give, give because I can, and because I should.
This energy I so willingly give away, and in doing so I am good.

Being good doesn't replenish what I have lost,
I bleed, and I cry, I have to pay the cost.

If ever I do not have enough for the task at hand,
They will come at me again and again.

I need it too, I beg and I plead,
They only see their strife, they are blind to my needs.

Everyday I must get every single thing done,
In this life I ask where is the fun.

Where is the me that laughs so hard the tears fall,
I gave my energy to play to you all.

I gave myself, energy bleeds from my veins,
My heart calls out for some to be saved before it all drains.

As if my guts have been spilled on the ground,
My energy is lowered to nothing I scream, but
nobody hears a sound.

I want what is mine, this energy is not yours,
you cannot simply take all that I have stored.

The Wrong Path

We have no guide for this life,
Lessons and rewards, gratitude and strife.

No line has been imprinted for all to follow,
Condemned to walk alone, at times feeling
hollow.

Outstretched hands we have grasped,
seldom do they remain, somethings just can't
last.

We go through every season, causing all the
emotions,
Always looking for silence to whisk away our
minds commotion.

Others we feel are weaker, judgemental thoughts
linger.

Why has she done this, doesn't she know,
There was an easier way for her to go.

He has no compassion for others, he has even
turned on his brothers.

No matter where you now stand, you were only
given the cards in your hand.

The wrong path has before lead people to what
is right,
Just as the right path has lead people to
nightmares each night.

So the path you walk is yours no exceptions, we
are not to judge others on their life lessons.

What Would It Be Like

Buzz the bee announces to the hive, such hard
work to keep so many alive.

Looking out at the tree that holds his home, how
can it stand for so long and be so alone.

What would it be like,
If this were my life.

A tree grows big and strong, wondering what it
must endure and for how long.

It watches the water flow, from the river giving
it nutrients from below.

What would it be like,
If this were my life.

The river rages, flowing far,
Until it reaches this beautiful farm.

Always moving, always seeing change,
wondering if it could be happy with a stationary
stage.

What would it be like,
If this were my life.

A horse pulling his plow,
Wondering what happens now.

Could I be a farmer the next time around, my
only source to live off being the ground.

What would it be like,
If this were my life.

We move from life to life without knowing,
From where we came or where we are going.

Hold On

I cannot stay in this way,
It doesn't matter where I go, or what I say.

I have to find my ground,
I have looked everywhere, but you aren't around.

Am I that out of reach, or have you all moved
further, what lesson are you trying to teach.

This is me, I am still the same, somewhere
behind the pointing fingers, behind all the
blame.

I am not trying to pretend I'm innocent at all, I'm
just trying to find the grasp that won't let me fall.

I need you, I begged, maybe you couldn't hear
my cry, I flailed my arms, still calling out, I
should have came straight to you asking why.

But I couldn't, how could I even ask, for some
reason I thought you weren't up for the task.

Trying got me nowhere even close to where I needed to be. All I asked is that just one single person actually hold onto me.

Your Guide

People sometimes come into my life, but they do
not stay.
No matter how much I try to hold on, and I
know it has to be this way.

Not everyone has a permanent place, some only
have a season.
It is because they were to teach me a lesson, they
were there for a reason.

I am the one who sometimes walks away. It is
part of my growth.
For the span of a lifetime, we have to remember
nobody holds an oath.

Not to you or me, the truest of promises don't
always stay true.
Like leaves in the autumn, some fall away, no
longer connected to you.

We must rejoice the love and laughter shared,
and learn to let go.
Do not reach for them, when it has passed your
heart will know.

You will be okay, let the pain settle, and find the happiness inside.
As you move throughout this life, you will have all the lessons as your guide.

Kindness Along The Road

Life is just one long road, everyone walks it, but no path is like another.
We each face different tribulations, so many stripes of color.

I cannot console your pain completely, I haven't faced the same demons.
As you cannot hold my hand, we fought for different reasons.

We can stand united in the fact that struggle is real,
It stays with us through the length of our lives, something we always feel.

This road is treacherous, long, and wary for some.
Others do not have a long travel, early on their time will come.

Even side by side we can be miles apart.
Because we do not see the shadows in another's heart.

No matter where on this road you may stand.
There are situations you will find you cannot understand.

This is where kindness is key.
Because it will take nothing from you, and nothing from me.

Glass Heart

I take every piece of myself and shove it inside,
tucked away.
It keeps me numb, emotions neutralized. Speak
up you say.

The words can't escape, blocked by a glass wall.
I cannot simply be myself, not even a little, not
at all.

I cannot ask you to fix everything that I have
made disappear.
I do not want to open myself, how do I make
that clear?

Everything must be just so, for it to fit inside my
heart.
Taking pieces out will end in disaster, it could all
fall apart.

Bottling it up isn't always safe, it has shattered
before.
I will only let it effect me, there is no harm to
you as I pick the pieces off the floor.

My heart isn't flesh like yours, we are not the same.
Mine is made of glass, I know because of the pain.

See when it breaks it's impossible to have a clean start.
I still feel the shards left inside this empty cavity that used to hold my heart.

Living Lives

Sit down, relax, release the troubles of today.
How have you been, what's wrong, are you okay?

Today's battles are over, take time to be strong.
The battle will be over soon, I promise it won't be long.

Have you found happiness inside this life?
I hope you have, nobody deserves so much strife.

Do you see your accomplishments before you, all that you have done?
I'm so proud of you for pushing so hard, and allowing yourself some fun.

I am sorry for the heartbreaks you had to face.
It is nice to see that you healed your heart at your own pace.

The work you have done was so important to others too.
See some might have not overcome their obstacles without you.

Is there anything you feel was not fulfilled this time?
Something you might want to take, something to keep in mind.

Where would you like to be in the next lesson you face?
Who do you feel you need to bring with you to that place?

I know you have just finished another death.
But still we must choose the next life's last breath.

Do you see the lessons and life that you chose?
If you agree, let's bring this to a close.

Whenever you are ready, please come along with me.
Good luck, I hope your life brings you everything you need.

When I Cannot Remember

How long must I stay inside this fog, memories tucked away for too long.

I miss me, I miss you, I miss remembering the life I had. I cannot remember important things, my soul knows, and that's why sometimes I am sad.

It is frustrating when I cannot seem to place something I just held a few moments ago, yelling at me will not help me remember, it only causes me to feel like a failure.

I'm failing at life every single day, I do not need the constant reminder. Just be here to hold my hand the way you know I held yours.

Although I cannot find the place scenes from my life are hiding, when I have those moments of clarity please take time to reminisce with me.

It makes my broken heart whole, and I am able to laugh and cry. Those are the times that I shine inside.

Nobody knows when the past will be erased, gone forever, never again to surface. So please take the time while I shine.

I will need you even when who you are isn't clear, that is when the fruits of my unconditional love will bloom.

Guiding and loving a parent of whom you are now a stranger cannot be easy, and it will break your tender heart.

But I hope for you it is also rewarding, taking care of them the way they did you from the start.

Hold my hand through this storm that will not fade, for I loved, cared, and hurt in those days that have gone away.

Matching My Heart

Living every single day faking all the emotions, because unlike you I do not fit.

I do not fit inside this body that was created just for me. I do not fit inside the box somebody else checked.

I feel like a failure, because I simply cannot be me, I could if you would try to look through something other than your rose colored glass.

Understand that everything cannot be black and white, there's an entire gray area in which I reside.

Am I okay you ask, inside I scream 'no I'm not, please see me', but my only reply is "yea, I'm fine" because I feel you aren't ready.

You aren't ready to see the truth, you aren't ready to see me, you aren't ready to hear the words I have been keeping inside, the same ones that are killing me.

I am not the version of myself you have known from the start, I can no longer pretend to match my parts, I have to match my heart.

One day I'll be brave enough to stand up and force myself to say the words, so I can for the first time in my life be heard.

I trust you will understand and love me for the real me. Because who you thought I was isn't who I am.

Please do your best to understand, because living my truth is important, shoving it inside is how I could become unalive.

Who I Am

I am all you have, without me you wouldn't know from where you came, or where you are going.

I have the answers to lessons, and to the questions you seek. All you have to do is trust in me.

I have held onto your life thus far, and I will keep holding on as far as your path will go.

Sometimes I might put you through trouble, I do not mean to, I am sorry it hurt, but sometimes it is you who spoke the words first.

I hold all the happiness, and pain, everything that has happened in your beautiful life. I try to stay positive, as I am your guide.

Think of something wonderful, think of something that let's melancholy creep inside. From where did those things come from, they came from me, for I am your mind.

Child Inside

I am still here, I am deep inside, your inner child cried.

I like to laugh and play, I like feeling free. It is how I cope with things that scare me.

I see, and I feel, I cannot escape when I am afraid. I just trust that you are doing what's best, I never feel betrayed.

I just want you to remember I am a child, somethings are too much. Sometimes I would like you to keep me in mind, you do not have to rush.

Think back on your life, the things that you have gone through. I never left, all of those things I felt too.

You have grown into a bigger version of myself, but here I stay frozen as a child, the smaller version of yourself.

Sometimes deep inside you want to cry. That is me, please release the tears, that is how I cope with all of these fears.

When you lash out for no reason at all, I am trying to understand something difficult. Those things that are even hard for you as an adult.

Just remember to play when you feel the urge, maybe dance in the rain. That is how I release these big feelings, that is how you can help me stay safe.

Fly

As a parent the most important thing you can do is lift up your children.

Lift them up from a nightmare safe inside your arms, remember to tell them how much you will fight to keep them from harm.

Lift them up after they scraped their knee, tell them your kisses will make it better, your love is the best medicine.

Lift them up after they had a bad day, don't forget to listen to everything they are wanting to say.

Lift them up when they struggle, it's ok to tell them that you have struggled too. Knowing this can help them to realize it happens, they are not a failure.

Lift them up when they make little or big strides, notice their accomplishments. Help them believe they can fly.

Your child's confidence comes from home, make sure you are present so they won't have to feel alone.

Whether your child is standing high and strong, or walking through hell, they always need your guidance, please be their stepping stones to be better in life.

Caged

I can never take back my actions, I cannot be what you needed then. I can only stand and hope I am what you need now.

The past is behind us, but it is not forgotten. The words that should have never been said, the actions that cut so deep.

I didn't mean it, and if I did I probably didn't say it right. See I'm not perfect and I have been wrong.

But everyday is a chance to be better, everyday is my chance to rebuild what was.

When I was younger I burned bridges, the same ones I didn't know I would desperately wish for someday.

I do not have the tools to fix it, and if I do I probably don't know how to use them right.

Pain, betrayal, fear, the things I have done, the things I have caused. For what, or why you ask. Because I didn't know.

I didn't know who I was, I was selfish, I didn't consider the cost.

Damn it I'm sorry, but that is all I can say. Because all of the words that should be coming are trapped behind my ego.

The part of me that is ok saying I screwed up, but cannot move passed that, I'm frozen.

I fear you will see me as I do, my hatred towards myself will bleed into your heart. The same as the wounds I inflicted because of something you didn't do.

So I'm sorry, and you know for what, don't make me say it. Because if I do it will become mine, I'll own it.

I know that is screwed up and you need the words to be said, but I can't, I won't. That's on me.

See I haven't changed, not even a little. I'm trying to be the person you need, but I cannot cut off my arms to mend your heart.

So here are my pointless ramblings, the things I still can't admit. And I'm even sorry for that, I'm sorry for everything.

Someday when I'm stronger, and truly changed,
I will stand in front of you and open your cage.

Your Home

When we first met I saw endless opportunities,
everything was about to begin.
We found each other, that in itself was a miracle.
I knew I had everything you needed within.

All the new brought happiness neither of us
could ignore.
We had this place to grow and learn, a life full of
experiences to explore.

I watched as you opened your heart, the beauty
of your bloom.
I wanted so badly to take away any pain, the
things I knew I couldn't exhume.

So many years we shared this place, I loved the
memories together we made.
I was full, I hoped your heart was too. The
thought of you leaving left me afraid.

Had I been everything you truly needed all this
time?
You were straying, I felt it in my heart, it
consumedmy mind.

Your search for happiness no longer held you to me.
I had no choice, but to let you go, to let you be free.

As I watched you pack away our life together.
I yearned for what was, when we could have had forever.

I couldn't stop you as you walked out, no matter how much I wanted us here.
It's not because I didn't have the fight in me, it wasn't even because of fear.

It was because I am only a house, but I thought I would always be your home.

A Good Book

Come into the library, to take a look, searching cover to cover for that perfect book.

You pick me up and read a few lines here and there, then set me back down without a care.

I know I'm good, full of stories of laughter, that would make the reader wonder what comes after.

But here I sit, never being selected. A wholesome book being neglected.

Watching as others leave with you, but I stand firm to what I know is true.

After years of waiting you finally gives me the time, but I feel it is too late I cry.

For I am no longer new, and I know I won't be good to you.

For my words have faded, I am past my prime, I could have been good, oh how I did shine.

Pieces of me fall to the ground as you turn page after page. You hold me as a treasure, as you guess my age.

I never wanted to be old, I never wanted to fall apart, I only wanted desperately to fill someone's heart.

My life I spent waiting for you, to find me and bring me home, I stayed on that shelf to feel alone.

Although I'll be thankful for you selecting me, I just wish it was before my story became empty.

Half of Me is She

Have you ever felt so full,
Like nothing was missing from your soul.

Living your life not knowing yourself,
Tucking things you couldn't understand on the highest shelf.

I didn't know what I would one day find,
My higher self lead me where I had been blind.

My friend I confided in over years,
The only one to calm my loudest fears.

A realization crept, crawling, consuming me,
I began to realize I held the key.

Time went by, this stayed up high out of reach,
Until my heart, mind, and soul was ready to seek.

Half of Me is she, and half of she is me.

One soul split to learn lessons faster,
Than ever a single life could master.

My Masks

You say you know me, but how can that be true?
You see, I never even showed myself to you.

Not really, not the core of who I am. I learned
early to tip toe, that is how it began.

I read emotions, and if judgment is what you
portray, that is when I know myself must be
tucked away.

A facade of masks hang on my wall, the ones I
know won't let me fall.

It is draining to say the least, always walking on
the brim, wishing that just once I can let others
in.

I have to be who you want to see. I cannot
simply be me.

It isn't fair to myself, it isn't the truth, but I'm not
fake I promise. I'm as real as I can be with you
on the surface.

I'm in here, I'm ready to be free, just once I would love to let everything fall. But I am not myself even inside, not even at all.

Voices Unheard

Have you heard it, it is closer than you would believe. It is in the quiet, in the shadows, do not be decieved.

A cry asking to be heard, a cry that cannot make even one word.

You have to listen to the silence that carries a different sound. The silence that you hear when you come around.

A child without a voice, a child without love. A child who isn't given what they need. These children are neglected the way that shows, everything looks fine, although they bleed.

They aren't given the basics to survive, it is a wonder they are strong enough to be alive.

What children need isn't truly food, water, and a home. In their heart they need to know they aren't alone.

They need kisses, and hugs, all of the love. Not just the words to be said. They need to feel it in their soul, this is something that can't be fed.

So many kids do not have the true love that others do. The kind that puts them before you.

So please listen to the voices that you cannot hear. The ones that you do not even know are near.

The World Around

Have you seen a butterfly disover its wings,
have you heard the music that the wind sings.

Birds chirping is a beautiful sound, this
communication we haven't found.

The world is more alive than you could believe.
You have to learn to feel more than you see.

It is all yours, it is there if you know the
questions to ask. It's listening to the world's
heart beat, this is not a simple task.

You have to learn that everything feels the way
you do. The grass, the rivers, everything is
trying to vibrate with you.

Learn to listen, words they don't speak, use the
energy that is there for you to seek.

We are all alive, and in tune. Everything is
connected by a tether.
Sparking, and radiant, a level of life you cannot
measure.

Find a place to sit on the ground, close your eyes and just breathe. It is open to you, trying hard to pull you into everything.

I Did It

I have thrown all these words on paper, but not for you, this is for me.

So I can feel like I accomplished something, a task that isn't even daunting.

Deadlines and I aren't compatible, not at all. As soon as I see that date, I set myself up to fall.

So I spit everything inside out, and hope I can make it in time.

I could write twenty poems a day, if I didn't have a reason. It's getting closer I say as I search through what I rejected.

The basket of poems that weren't good enough, the pile of random thoughts I figured could make it.

Page after page, my heart bleeds through my pen to make ink.

I'm desperate to force my mind to find enough words. Somewhere inside is something that has never been heard.

You can't do this, man you are cutting it close. But I keep spewing out something to fill these pages.

Even a poem about writing poems, man they are going to think you are grasping.

I am, I am grasping to prove to myself that I can do this, just this once.

Meet the finish line with a book, one I've written from my very soul.

So when you read this know I did it, I finally finished on time. This is me, and this is mine.

www.ingramcontent.com/pod-product-compliance
Lightning Source LLC
Chambersburg PA
CBHW051745130826
49812CB00033B/1016
* 9 7 8 9 3 5 7 2 1 0 8 5 0 *